Breaking Through To God

The Way of the Cross

D1547333

LADISLAUS BOROS

Breaking Through To God
The Way of the Cross

Translated by
PETER HEBBLETHWAITE S.J.

Darton, Longman & Todd Ltd

© 1973 Darton, Longman and Todd Ltd.,
originally published as
Durchbruch zu Gott
by Verlag Gerhard Kaffke
Bergen–Enkeim, Frankfurt/Main
West Germany

ISBN 0 232 51222 1

Illustrations by
Evamaria Brüchner-von-Eiff

ACKNOWLEDGEMENTS

The Publishers acknowledge with gratitude the permission
of The National Council Churches of America to quote
various passages from the Revised Standard Version of the
Bible.

Printed Offset Litho in Great Britain by
Cox & Wyman Ltd, London, Fakenham and Reading

Contents

Introduction

There are many different ways of making the Stations of the Cross. The best of all consists simply in contemplating our suffering Lord and pondering in the heart how much pain and distress he bore on our behalf. Yet that is not the method we will follow here. When one makes the effort to understand Christ's existence in the light of one's own experiences, avoiding familiar and ready-made ideas, then his way to God becomes more intelligible, more meaningful.

One thing we must grasp clearly from the outset: God became man, and *as man* had to win through to God. There was a thoroughly genuine human development in his life. In that sense there was nothing unusual in the Way of the Cross: it was simply the way in which Christ had to realise his human individuality in our world. Incarnation and Redemption in this context mean that God has entered fully into our human situation.

But in the Way of the Cross, Christ also shows how man can come to God: through judgement and defeat to resurrection. If I have managed to present in a credible way this underlying pattern of faith, which applies to all mankind, then I have done what I set out to do. Christians and non-Christians too can find here an opportunity to grow in spiritual perception. And then the meditation on the Passion of Christ will indeed be an example of 'the piety of the intellect'.

L.B.
Zürich

Judged

Within a single night
Christ was betrayed by a friend,
abandoned and denied by his disciples,
struck in the face, cast into prison,
mocked, condemned.
The Passion of Christ begins
with an act of *betrayal*.
Yet till the end Christ
continues to call Judas Iscariot 'Friend'.
None of the Apostles,
and certainly none of us,
has the right to feel superior to Judas.
We have all, in one way or another, already betrayed
friends.
But the contrary is also true :
someone whom we love can poison our life.
To love with honour and in a mature way
is therefore always a matter
of following Christ along the way of the cross.

After betrayal came *abandonment*.
As Christ is arrested all the disciples run away.
Yet the breakthrough of humanity to God
can only happen in Christ;
and there are decisive moments in human life
which we must shoulder alone, bear in solitude.

Then Christ is *struck in the face*.
That is written in the Gospels.
He was fully man,
which means that when his body was struck,
his soul too suffered.
Anyone who strikes Christ attacks his soul.
But at the same time, he was God-man.
So anyone who wounds the body of Christ,
injures his soul, and beyond that, strikes at God.
By taking humanity on himself,
Christ became vulnerable.
All of us have wounded and injured our fellow men.

Finally Christ is *condemned*.
By entering fully into our ordinary human existence,
he exposed himself to feel
the keenest pain that a human being can suffer :
the sacrifice of our uniqueness.
This sacrifice, along with abandonment to loneliness,
is the worst pain.

Pilate and Herod

Christ was handed over to the political authorities.
Pilate was quite tolerant towards him.
But Christ's misfortune gave him a chance
to go on playing a political game.
He sent Christ to Herod.
The life of Christ was broken
on two men of power.
He acted out a sort of living parable
in which we can all recognise
our own experience.

First the experience of *insincerity*.
Pilate was a sophisticated, cultivated man.
That is why his question –
'What is truth?' –
is so staggering for us,
because it is not asked in a spirit of
restless seeking after the truth,
but with a tone of blasé indifference.
In a self-seeking world
what is straight can become crooked
and what is crooked, straight.
But then freedom, humility, friendship and love
become impossible.
Being becomes non-being,
truth unimportant
and man a cultivated, hollow puppet.

In such a topsy-turvy, perverted world,
Christ who was Truth itself, could expect only one fate:
crucifixion.

Then Christ was *mocked*.
Before Herod Christ is still more defenceless
than before Pilate.
It seems that Herod was
a rather pathetic person,
interested in
the odd, the absurd, the unusual.
Perhaps he thought:
This prophet could perform some spectacular tricks
and help to relieve my boredom.
But before Herod Christ remains silent.
He says nothing.
Not a word.

We have to ask ourselves frankly:
How dare we reduce another human person
to an object of amusement.
Yet that often happens.
We expect others to amuse or divert us
even if it makes them miserable.
What took place at Herod's court
is something we can all experience.
And, if one has grasped
what it really means to be a man,
to be mocked is to be mortally wounded.
Thus detail by detail
the cross of Christ is built
into the stuff of our human existence.

Jesus falls

Jesus conceals his divine nature.
If he had once allowed his power
to shine forth,
he could have saved himself much suffering.
But he did not
because he wanted as God to undergo
everything that we as men
have to undergo.
He broke through
into the realm of our suffering.
This should be a hint for us :
In distress do not look
for the easiest way out,
bear your trials.
You will never be happy
if you seek only happiness for yourself.
To take up one's cross
is not really difficult;
what is difficult,
and the real cross,
is that patient endurance
which lasts a lifetime.

Those men who wield power (says Christ)
cannot touch me.
I do not bear any grudge against them.
But I am critical of them

when they are blinded by their success
and their power over others.
I do not want to intervene
on my own behalf.
Don't make it too easy for yourself.
My grace is not given
to make things easier
but so that you may still hope,
when apparently all hope has been
dashed to the ground
and when you feel broken.
Then you must try
to rise up again.

If you are a Christian
do not be arrogant
or over-confident.
A Christian is not
a triumphalist.
Christ is now empty, burnt out.
He can go no farther
and he falls to the ground.
That is why we must always remember,
when the suffering seems unbearable,
to do exactly what Christ does.
We should admit
that we are beaten
and make a gift
of our opened heart.
It is a hard way
and it can seem impassable;
but the hardness of God
is the gentleness of Christ.
The gentleness of Christ

breaks into our human existence
and makes us,
even in unbearable suffering,
capable of happiness.

Meeting Mary

Mary realised in her everyday life
the purpose for which Christ undertook
the painful way of the cross:
a completely limpid human life.
Hers is a love that goes directly to its goal.
In such a life
there is no double-think, no falsity,
and God can make his home there.
He can be so closely bound to her
that he comes as her baby.
In Mary life
is lived to the full.
This most alive of human beings
is granted once more
the grace of a meeting with Christ.

The deep meaning of this encounter
is that Christ dies for those
who are like Mary.
Of course he also died
for all men;
the reward is the same for all.
But here there is no question of reward.
What counts is this limpidity, uprightness.
It is found in those who shun
lies and duplicity, and the abuse of power.
Christ deprives no one of happiness.
What happened in the end

to Judas, Pilate and Herod
concerns only Christ.
But what Christ brought to life
in the soul of Mary
is the sketch of our future.
There something precious came into being :
humanity redeemed.

And that is the ultimate meaning
of this way of the cross :
God directs human life
towards heaven.
Into a development lasting
millions of years,
which is crowned when
the energy of the universe
is concentrated in man,
God enters,
becomes man himself,
goes forward to his death,
and shatters the limiting walls
of this world.
And through the breach we glimpse
eternal fulfilment.
Only one who believes
in the cross of Christ,
can bring hope to our world.
Mary realises in herself,
decisively, the fullness of the human,
and routs all the forces
of dispersal and dishonour.
She is the mother of all,
because she was the mother of Christ
on the way of the cross.

Helped

Once more Christ is alone.
The soldiers picked out of the crowd
a man called Simon,
as he was coming home from the fields.
They forced him to carry the cross
for Jesus.
Christ allows himself to be *helped*
by this stranger.

He probably felt:
why should I be concerned
any more about my own distress?
Give your life, as it ebbs away,
one final meaning:
let yourself be helped.
His life-work was over.
On all sides he found misunderstanding,
hostility, and, what is worse,
mockery.
Now the hand of a stranger
grasps him.
At long last there is
a friendly presence by his side.
Such moments can occur
in the varied situations of our life.
Moments of disappointment
or of failure.

Moments in which we are fully aware
of the meaninglessness of our existence;
Moments in which we ask God,
whether it were better
had we never been born;
At such times we can learn from
the attitude of Christ:
He lets himself be helped
by a stranger.

And so he is saying to us:
When you suffer,
seek someone out,
don't cut yourself off.
Let yourself, from time to time,
be sustained by others.
Someone seeking consolation
evokes compassion, mercy.
To seek human consolation
is a Christian duty.
You should have enough courage
to allow the other
to share your suffering.
Christ's suffering was a gift to the world.
Follow him along this way
and he will show you how to become
fully yourself.

Becoming like Him

Veronica stands before Jesus
and offers him a linen towel.
Every man receives from Jesus
the grace to follow him
and become like him:
all human beings,
precisely because they are human,
have to carry their cross.
When a man consents
freely and willingly
to his cross,
then he is a Christian.
That is the way it is
and must be.

I accept my cross
because my Lord
has done likewise.
This is the way
the lordship of Christ
is established in our world.

An authentic human existence
comes into being
only when man accepts
an *absolute claim*.

For us, this absolute
is Christ himself.
In the end all men
fail and are broken;
but Christians can accept this
in love.

Christian life
does not consist in inculcating
a set of principles,
but in the following
of a Person.

The courage to ask Christ
to share with us his attitudes,
even in humiliations
– or at the very least
to aspire towards that –
is the courage
to be a Christian.

To recognise
the overriding claim
of what is greater
is the only way
to greatness.
And yet this following of Christ
is no extraordinary thing :
every man will find the cross
somewhere along his path,
sometime.

À Christian is one who
consciously or implicitly
says *yes*, Amen, to the following
of Christ.

Weakness

Under the weight of the cross
Christ collapses
a second time.
We can link this fall
with his agony
in the garden.

Only three friends shared closely
in his suffering.
Christ laid a fearsome burden
on them and they broke down
under it.
'You will all fall away
because of me this night'
he says in Saint Matthew,   (26, 31)
who adds : 'He began to be
sorrowful and troubled'.   (26, 34)
Mark is even more insistent :
'He began to be
greatly distressed and troubled'.   (14, 33)
And Luke says that Christ was
'in agony'.
His life had become
a single cry of distress,
so much so that
'his sweat became like
great drops of blood
falling upon the ground'.   (23, 44)

His courage hesitated,
trembled out of fear;
his love was exposed
to abandonment by God.
In his powerless state
he fell to the ground,
cried out to his Father,
seemed to refuse the task ahead,
wandered forsaken
among the dark shadows
of the olive trees.

Three times
he addressed his Father
and said the same thing:
he could bear no more.
With weary unrecognising eyes
he glimpsed the Angel
sent to comfort him.
In the end, he managed
to consent,
but only after
a phrase of refusal:
'If thou art willing,
remove this cup from me,
nevertheless not my will,
but thine, be done'.   (Luke 23, 42)
Finally he could bear no more
and he cried out
'That is enough'.
What should he do now?
He had fallen to the ground,
cried out, sweated blood,
but he had held on.

Nothing glorious here,
nothing brave;
but he held on
in weakness, and perhaps,
in what we are tempted to call
cowardice.
But he held on.
Glory and bravery
are not the measure
of what it is to be human.
Man can fulfil his life
also in weakness.

Merciful

'And there followed him
a great multitude of the people,
and of women
who bewailed and lamented him.
But Jesus turning to them said:
"Daughters of Jerusalem,
do not weep for me,
but weep for yourselves
and your children"'.   (Luke 23: 27–28; RSV)

Mercy is love's readiness
to be seized
by another's suffering.
Christ does not refuse mercy.
He always took human distress
seriously;
he never closed his ears
to the cries of those who suffer.
It is perhaps Saint John
who most clearly
enables us to enter into
the compassion of Christ.
He shows how on the death of his friend,
Lazarus,
all the emotions of Christ
were aroused and engaged.
Yet Christ knew that he could not

banish all suffering
or wave it away
with a magic wand.

As Redeemer, his mission was not
to abolish suffering,
but rather to undergo,
transform and sanctify suffering.
Redemption means
the *disclosure of a new possibility*
precisely at the point where
our human nature
can do no more.

Yet his compassion
impels him to help and heal;
but his hands are tied
by his divine task.
Here an abyss opens up,
and the more we gaze into it,
the more we tremble
at the sense of awe
evoked by Christ.
It is the driving force of love
which makes the merciful
suffer.
In this way and in our world
suffering and love
are conjoined,
so that one cannot love
without humbly taking upon oneself
suffering.

But the hearts of those who love
are also the most humble:
they make a gift of their love
until almost nothing is left.

Suffering

Jesus falls to the ground
a third time.
Theologians tell us that Christ
lived in the state
of original justice.
They mean that there was no gap
between what he was
and what he did:
in all his dealings
he was fully himself.
In Christ,
who had to endure
the rough edges of existence,
this led to a frightening conclusion:
Not only did he feel suffering,
he *became* suffering.
But we must add that Christ
as man enjoyed
the immediate vision
of the Father.
God was the whole context
of his life.
What happens, then,
when suffering
breaks into such a life?
There follows a disturbance
of the senses and the feelings.
God himself

sacrifices endless beatitude
and so experiences to the full
the distance of God.

Thus Christ,
to a degree which for us
is unimaginable,
descends into hell,
into destruction without end.
There was no *consoling* closeness
of God at this moment;
only a closeness to God
in terror.

Often we fail to understand
what it meant to Christ
to be our Redeemer.
Without ever having fallen into sin,
he is exposed to the consequences
of sin.
His whole being is weighed down
by the sordidness of humanity.
And he comes through it all.
He fell to the ground,
to the sin-stained earth,
embraced it,
buried himself in it,
sought there shelter
from his Father.
Never yet has a man suffered
as Christ did.

Stripped

Christ is stripped
of his clothing.
God is stripped.
What can that mean?
God: the name we give
to the ineffable.
God: he who can never be pieced together
out of the realities
of this world.
God: before whom
our speech and thinking
fail.

Yet: *God is stripped*.
Surely he is Someone
who is infinitely above
change and passivity.
That idea of God is
splendid and powerful,
but it is also wrong.

The God of revelation
comes and goes,
prepares the future, leaves us,
drags himself away.
If already our limited thinking

cannot cope with the idea of 'God',
it is even more perplexed and helpless
when it meets a God
who *becomes*.
The perplexity and helplessness increase:
God is stripped.

The encounter with this God
is painful.
Job complained:
'How long wilt thou not
look away from me,
nor let me alone
till I swallow my spittle?'   (Job: 7, 19)
Now God himself undergoes
the same experience.
A man stands before us
trembling with fear,
on the verge of death.
He does not deserve this.
In his life he is so committed
to us and our humanity,
that Saint Paul,
shaken to the core,
can cry out:
'If we are faithless,
he remains faithful –
for he cannot deny himself'.   (2 Tim: 2, 13)

From now on
we shall be unable to think
of anything human,
except sin,

which does not also
apply to God.
Christ embodies
all that is beautiful
on earth.
But now he stands before us his face
covered with blood,
deeply disturbed
and riven by anxiety.
Is that 'the radiance of beauty'?
Our answer must be yes,
for he has truly given his all.

Crucified

'Behold the wood of the cross
on which hung the Saviour of the world :
come, let us adore him.'
This is what the Church sings
during the Good Friday liturgy.
Before the mystery of his death
on the cross,
we must fall silent.
Only *adoration* remains.
This fundamental letting go,
self-abandonment,
in the presence of God
is already adoration.
Not simply deep adoration
but the deepest possible.
Such adoration is like
pure light, clean air.
Through it breathes
unshakeable *trust*.
It comes from the conviction
that despite all difficulties
we are held in the hands of God.
As Jesus said in his last moments :
'Father, into thy hands,
I commend my spirit'.

All this should make us reflect seriously
on the fact that in our prayer

requests and thanks
and sometimes praise
are in the foreground,
while simple *adoration*
scarcely has a place.

Day by day so many impressions
and demands
crowd in upon us
that we can no longer stand
in simplicity of heart
beneath the cross
of our Saviour.
The pressures of everyday life
have edged God out.
We have to work ourselves free
so as to rediscover
living adoration
at the foot of the cross.
The power of Jesus was always gentle :
'He neither disputed nor quarrelled'.
He who said this of himself
was the one
to whom 'all power is given
in heaven and on earth'.   (Matt. 28, 18)

Perhaps we should also ponder
how Christ here
defends the sinner
against justice,
the defenceless
against those who wield power.
What he said to Peter

holds for all of us :
'Put your sword
back into its place'.   (Matt. 26, 52)
In Christ's death on the cross
a new world comes into being,
a world of disinterestedness,
of peace, of adoration.

Dying

Christ is now completely forsaken.
'My God, my God,
why have you abandoned me?'
After such words it is clear
that those we call 'atheists' or 'God-less'
cannot be our enemies,
but are rather those who undergo
precisely what Christ
suffered on the cross.
Only someone
who has felt himself to be
on the edge of the abyss,
can bring to them the gift
of infinite closeness.

Then from the parched throat of Christ
came the hoarse cry : 'I thirst'.
God begs us for help.
He asks for a mouthful of water.
In such moments
what we have to give
is irrelevant;
what counts is the attitude
that we express through our gift.
Thus into the world
there flows a vast peace,
a quiet companionship
with this God who suffers.

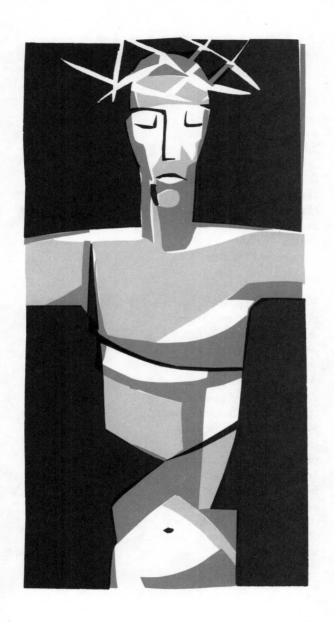

'It is consummated' said Jesus.
My hands and feet
are nailed to the cross.
I have surrendered
everything that was dear to me.
Now there is no more.
I can do no more.
The victory of Christ
is snatched
from the abyss of death.
He is now alone.
His final words give us
the key to this mystery:
'Father, into thy hands
I commend my spirit'.

Very little happened, apparently,
on and around this cross.
Another criminal hangs
between two others
who also died.
A few women wept.
A man tortured to death
spoke a few stammering words.
But he broke out beyond
this suffering
towards a distant horizon.
In his death agony
he spoke to every one of us
and said yes to everything
that makes us truly human.
Christ is our consent, our *Amen*,
to existence.

At Rest

Christ was taken down from the cross
and Mary took him in her arms.
What can her thoughts have been
as she saw her son lying there,
now at rest?
She must have looked back
over her own life.
As for each of us
her life was one of endless
growth and process.
It was filled with
the humdrum cares of simple people:
much concern about
what to eat,
a share of pain,
and some moments of joy.
This was how her life was measured out:
a life, in fact, of
deep happiness in God,
a life ruled by the
ordinary daily round
of weariness and exhaustion
and apparent emptiness.
Now it all seems
so trivial to her.

All this previous experience
comes together for Mary

in the God-forsaken cry of her son.
In the earliest account of the Passion,
according to Saint Mark,
that is the only recorded word
of Christ on the cross.
Perhaps Mary understood,
perhaps she did not fully understand
the cry: 'My God, my God,
why have you abandoned me?'
But she understood enough
to take her son, once again,
into her arms.

God can send such a person
as Mary into our world.
She will know happiness
in the service of God.
Mary was not shaken
in her conviction.
Perhaps she would have been shaken,
if she had been exposed to the forces
of total disorder,
and if it had to be so.
Yet even then,
with anxious face, back bent,
her life in ruins,
she would have known happiness.
But now, in this very moment,
and in the heart of Mary,
the world is broken open
to God.
In the end she awaits
one last gift from her son:
without ever for a moment

needing to deny the value
of her human existence,
she enters her eternal home.
She had understood the essential:
he who would save himself
must lose himself.

Buried

Christ was taken down from the cross,
laid in his mother's arms
and then buried.
He is now at peace.
His body is still there,
but his soul has already journeyed
into 'the heart of the world'.
He goes down to the depths,
to the deepest and most radical
level of reality
which forms the basic ground
of our world.
And as Christ in his death
attains the ground of the universe,
he is present to the whole
of pre-Christian mankind.
The world is no longer the same.
In all its depths
and inwardness
Christ dwells.
From now on every act of
dying to the world
is a going home
to Christ.

The working out of his death means
in practical terms

for us today
simply this:
every selfless act,
every help we give
our fellow men,
is already *faith*.
As he plunges into the depths of the world,
he creates for us a new context
of salvation.
In everything that is
humanly good,
there is an encounter with Christ,
and also the creation
of a world redeemed: heaven.
If we are not to reduce this mystery
to an abstraction,
we must grasp
with the heart
what these things mean
to Christ himself.
Christ can be discovered
in all things and in all events.
He is there all the time,
the eternally valid, supreme reality,
so that our own actions
participate in
the action of Christ.
This eternally valid supreme reality
shines through all our dreams,
all our aspirations, all our hopes.
And its name is
and was ever: Christ.
Thus man enters
upon joy without end.

Risen

In the Easter event
heaven is opened to us,
irrevocably.
This is the basic and dominant
Christian attitude:
its name from now on
will be hope.

The early Christian community
understood Jesus
as 'He who leads to life'
and as 'the Principle of a new world'.
All the experiences of life,
including suffering and death,
can be fitted into
this basic attitude.
In this way something radically new
enters our world,
new styles
of patience, endurance, understanding.
God wants to set us free
from the grip
of routine and dullness.
Not simply to experience joy,
but to *be joy*
is the costing task
of every fresh day.

But true joy can only be found
where joy is given to others.

Since the resurrection of Christ
the true test of our Christian existence
is the selfless gift of joy to others.
In this way every man,
whether baptised or not,
can experience
in his whole being
a foretaste of heaven.
And so the Christian's task
is to let the light of heaven
shine through human experience,
so that it becomes
transparent.

If we try to sum up the best
of our human experiences
– those moments
of peace, awe, wonder,
courage, aspiration,
above all, love and friendship –
then we can gain a shadowy idea
of what heaven is like.
The Christian's task is
to live on earth from heaven.
To experience heaven in faith,
to recognise it as the ultimate reality
of our lives,
to spend ourselves in faith
for our brothers :
that is what Christian witness means today.

Valete

Our God does not promise us an easy life. But he has at least promised us one thing: that we shall always be able to find him, even in times of great difficulty. Our faith makes us responsible for the world. It is an undertaking for the world. It works itself out in everyday things, but now God himself has entered our prosaic world which is our challenge and perhaps our cross. The Christian should not be afraid of apparent emptiness. Christ promised that from his heart would flow streams of living water. When we try, without selfishness and without strain, to keep ourselves open to the unmerited gift of God, then, even without our being aware of it, streams of grace and divine joy will overflow from our hearts.

Contemplative Prayer

by Thomas Merton

'Thomas Merton's last testament bears the heart of his own message of renewal . . . nothing could more directly redeem the times than a rekindling of these deepest ranges of prayer'. Douglas Steere in his introduction.

Letters from the Desert

by Carlo Carretto

'Carlo Carretto has given us a piece of spiritual writing which can be mentioned in the same breath as "The Cloud of Unknowning" and Dame Julian's "Revelations of Divine Love".' *Reconciliation Quarterly.*

Courage to Pray

by Metropolitan Anthony and Georges LeFebvre OSB

In this book the reader can savour the richness of the spirituality of both Eastern and Western Christendom and discover how much there is to learn from both traditions.

Christian Vocation

by Rene Voillaume

In the intelligible and unsentimental style which Voillaume has made his own, this book takes the form of a series of authentically contemplative meditations on the true meaning and nature of the Christian vocation.